Dare to Dream

Tween's Road to Success

Shervin A. Azar

Dedication

I dedicate this book to my mom and dad who have been truly an inspiration to me and gave me the idea of writing this book.

ISBN-10: 1539536378

ISBN-13: 978-1539536376

Price: $9.99 US | $12.99 CAN

CONTENTS

The Impossible Is Possible

Imagine that you're an eight-year-old immigrant boy who just moved to Canada with your parents; you have zero knowledge of the English language and no ability to communicate with other people except to say hello.

You can't even start a simple conversation with your teachers or classmates, and you've already begun to give up on yourself, knowing there is only the slightest chance that you will ever be able to speak English.

What would you do if you were in such a challenging situation?

Just think about it. Put yourself in my shoes. Imagine that you can't say a word of English, and then— only three years later—boom, you're writing a book! Doesn't that sound impossible? Well, guess what:

everybody once thought that going into outer space was impossible and making a device that would let you communicate with someone far away was similarly impossible.

But here's the thing—nothing is impossible! You can achieve anything you want if you just take tiny steps toward your goals. In fact, impossible is possible!

When I first came to Canada almost four years ago, at the age of eight, I thought it would be impossible to learn a new language, impossible to fit in to my new community, and impossible to be a Canadian. Due to my dad's job, we had to relocate and change our province three times in just two years. I had to face many challenges including readopting myself with a new school, new teachers, new friends and new environment. I would confess, that was very hard for me as an immigrant boy with poor English knowledge.

After only nine months living in Toronto, we moved to the east of Canada, New Brunswick and settled in the city of Moncton.

It was a new city and a new school for me, and I immediately started going to school after arrival. It was a whole new atmosphere, but I tried hard to catch up. To be honest, it was really frustrating for a kid at my age particularly at the first couple of months. I was nine years old at the time by the way.

Time passed and things were getting better for me, but that was not the end of the story. Another move was on the way. After just six months being in New Brunswick, one day my mom came to me and said: Shervin, we're about to have another move in a couple of months. This time we had to move to British Columbia. It was a big move, crossing the country from East to West but for me, the main concern was my few friends and my teachers that I had to leave so soon.

I was completely shocked. "No Mom! No more moving again" I said in a desperate voice. I remember, I really had had an unpleasant feeling for the first couple of weeks after that day, but I tried not to expose that in front of my parents. It took me a while that I learned, any challenge will come with a new gift as well, it makes us stronger and tougher.

Always be open for unpredicted challenges either in the school or personal life as it might lead you to discover your hidden capabilities and strengths. Now, when I look back to those days, despite all the difficulties, they've also given me at the same time tremendous experience and learning.

Eventually, we ended up in Abbotsford, a city located around seventy kilometers East of Vancouver.

Let me share something significant with you: if Steve Jobs had never come up with the revolutionary idea to make a really high-tech cell phone because he thought it was impossible to do so, then we would not have smartphones all over the world right now, changing our lives for the better. If scientists like Galileo had never taken action on their beliefs, then we would have never found out how big the universe is or that the earth is not at its center.

If I had said it was impossible for me to write this book, guess what would have happened. When you say something is impossible, your brain gets the message that anything you might try to do is equally impossible. After that, your brain locks into that way of thinking, and consequently, you will never be able to act against your mind-set.

So, if you're the kind of boy or girl who always assumes that the things you're trying or wanting to do are impossible, then I recommend that you rethink your habits. You have to pretend that there is no such word as *impossible* in the dictionary of success.

Now, you're probably wondering what happened when I first came to Canada, so let me tell you how this all started. I was about to go to elementary school in Toronto, even with my shivers and goose bumps and despite having no idea what I was getting myself into. It was right before Christmas, and I was already behind the rest of the class by almost four months.

I will never forget that first day. As I entered the classroom, everyone stared at me with their complete attention. I found out right away that it's really tough to be around others but not be able to communicate with them. Sometimes we have no other option than talking with our eyes rather than our mouth, and that's what I did for the first couple of months after I arrived.

I recall very well how the teacher said, "Hello, class! I would like you to welcome our new student, Shervin." That was when I used the only "magical" English word that I knew at the time.

"Hello," I said to the class, not too loudly. I received a few *hellos* from my classmates in return, which felt intimate and gave me a little bit of confidence. The teacher's introduction, which was really short, didn't do much at all to reduce my stress.

I didn't understand anything at all back then, but—luckily for me—there were three Iranian kids in my class, and they helped me a lot by translating everything for me.

I remember that I was so nervous, particularly in the first couple of months. I was afraid that I wouldn't fit in with my classmates or even fit in to their culture at all.

Now look at me. In three years, I have learned English this well, and as of this year, I have already started to learn French at a French immersion middle school. So now I'm getting to know my third language, and—to be honest—I'm really pumped for more. Just to inform you, I was born in Iran, so my first language is Persian. My parents and I most often use that at home to communicate with one another.

Well, you're probably wondering how I learned English so quickly that I could write a book. I will talk about that in a second—and it might be inspiring to many of you—but for now, I'm going to talk about how we came to live in this beautiful, fabulous country called Canada and what an adventure it was for us to get here.

In Toronto, we rented a cozy basement apartment that really wasn't big enough for the three of us—my mom, my dad, and me. But, even though it was kind of small, it was all that we could afford. For various reasons—including currency devaluation, economic problems, and international sanctions—we had not brought enough money to Canada.

We had lots of insects in our basement—disturbing ones that would literally freak you out. I will never forget all those creepy-crawlies that had one hundred feet along with four or six eyes! I confess that those bothered me the whole the time we lived there. Imagine that you're in your house, watching Medusa get beheaded in *Clash of the Titans*, when you suddenly look to the floor and see three cockroaches battling a really big house centipede.

We had a lot of centipedes in our house, and when I say *a lot*, you'll probably think I'm exaggerating, but—believe me—their numbers were infinite. In fact, most of the time when I brushed my teeth, a centipede would be right beside me, looking on. I always hesitated to kill them—but I always did!

When we went to Walmart, I was like, "Mom, which one should we buy—the 'best centipede killer in town' or the 'best centipede killer around'?"

Yeah, good times, good times. I mean, *horrible* times!

Imagine that you hadn't seen a caterpillar or centipede in your entire life and then you had a bunch of them living with you in your house! Would you want to live in a house like that? How would you be able to concentrate enough to learn a new language or deal with a new environment?

This is the part where I explain how I managed to learn English in less than three years—and how I did the impossible. But first, before you read on, I have to ask you something really important: On a scale of one to ten, how committed are you to changing and taking control of your life through reading this book? If your answer is higher than six, that's great news. It means that you are ready to step up and take action, and that you are eager for excellence.

I did not write this book just to get famous; I wrote it to share what I believe helped me to survive in critical situations and, on top of that, to actually change people's lives—particularly the lives of minors, as they are the ones with a long way ahead of them, full of opportunities and prospects. I could have easily *not* written this book, but I chose to share my perspective with you, as I believe that sharing knowledge is the only way to learn.

Crucial to my book is the belief that everything that happens to us is the result of the way we think. Our thinking causes our actions, and our actions shape our destiny. Whether that's good or bad, everything that will ever happen to us will be our responsibility.

So, if you are looking for a superior future, and especially if you're in or nearing the teenage age-group, you should learn how to control your thinking, as it is already significantly shaping your destiny.

Now, let's talk about a certain kind of law that affects every single one of us. It's cool and unique, and I'm sure that you can gain some major advantages if you learn how to use it.

The Law of Attraction

So you're probably thinking, "What the heck is the law of attraction?"

The law of attraction, or what some call the power of the universe, is a force beyond your imagination. You know about the law of gravity, the law of motion, and the law of mass. Well, the law of attraction is similar to those in that it has always been and will always be. It can't be created or destroyed.

Let me tell you how this power beyond your wildest dreams works. The movie *Aladdin* has a simple example of what the law of attraction does. I'll explain in case you haven't seen it. A guy named Aladdin finds a lamp—an "empty" lamp. He rubs the dust off of it to clean it, and suddenly, a genie comes out of it. The genie always—and I mean *always*—says, "Your wish is my command." Like a genie who grants your wishes, the law of attraction delivers whatever you want, think, or feel, over and over again.

For instance, let's say that Jimmy is a soccer player and somebody tackles him. He says, "Oh, come on! Why did this happen to me?" or "It could have happened to somebody else!" or even "Like, why would you do that?" Now, I think you know that he is attracting negativity, and you know what the law of attraction says: "Your wish is my command." From now on, he will probably continue to get tackled.

As the saying goes, "whatever you're thinking and feeling today is creating your future." Now you see that you don't want to be a negative person, because otherwise, you will attract only negative things, and that will cause nothing but misery. That's why you have to be careful of how you think and feel.

If you are the kind of youth who carries negativity with you in your daily life most of the time, in your personal relationships with either your friends in school or your parents or siblings at home, then I highly recommend that you adopt a more positive thinking style. Trust me, a negative attitude will bring lots of frustration and awfulness into your life, and it won't only influence your future success, but it will also affect your psychological and emotional well-being. Let's face it, when you're a negative person, none of your emotions work in the right way, and that will damage both your soul and mind. So don't be that person, OK?

Another really bad thing about being negative is that it will make you doubt yourself. It will take you down and won't let you raise yourself up. It will cause you to underestimate your capabilities, skills, and talents.

As the famous expression says, "stay away from negative people. They have a problem for every solution." What this means is that instead of finding a solution to any given problem, these people will always bring up a problem with any possible solution.

Once you're a positive person, however, the whole world will be fun. So try it out!

If you ask the people closest to me, they will tell you I'm a really fun guy and that I don't take the world seriously at all, ever. You know, I am this way because I think that life is simple—but we make it complicated. If you want to take life seriously, then life will mean nothing more to you than survival.

Have you ever said, for instance, "Argh! I can't study, I failed the boss battle on my game, and my shoes are ripped"? See, those are the little things in life that often concern you. But what you don't see from your perspective is that life is full of bigger problems. And the more you see those little things as big problems, the more the big problems will become like boss battles. What you want to do is find the root of your negativity and resolve it.

Let's say that your parents want McDonald's for lunch but you want Thai food. Trust me, you've been in this situation—when you're in the car with your parents, trying to decide where you're all going to eat, and you're like, "Mom and Dad, I really want Thai food," but then your mother tells you, "No, son, we're going to McDonald's." Suddenly, your father says, "Actually, we're going to Boston Pizza." After a couple of seconds, all of you are looking at each other angrily, and without warning, World War III starts with everybody screaming at, hitting, and even killing one another. If you think I'm exaggerating, then think again.

How am I not exaggerating? Well, think about this: How many times have humans started wars over arguments that came from their general negativity toward simple matters? No, just think about it. When a human does something bad, it's a result of his or her negativity and misunderstanding.

Why do you think Hitler had so much hatred? When he was a child, he had a really poor relationship with his father. He wanted to study fine arts, but his father badly wanted him to do something else. When he was sixteen years old, he quit school because his grades were continuously declining. He even lived homeless on the streets at one point. Just imagine that! What I am trying to tell you is that Hitler had all that negative energy and all that hatred, and he released it on the Jews during World War II, which led to the destruction of much of the world and its people.

Anyway, when you have that kind of negativity, try to find its root and replace it with a positive attitude. Believe me, you can do it—just give it a shot.

Again, if you and your parents can't agree on where to eat, don't get angry! A game of rock-paper-scissors might help you to decide which place to go to—or you could just let everyone get the kind of food that they want at a regular, all-inclusive restaurant and then sit together to enjoy your meals. It's that easy.

Now, don't tell me that your problem doesn't have a solution. There is always a solution to every problem, even if sometimes it's a funny one—like rock-paper-scissors!

According to the law of attraction, when you wish for something badly and are really positive about it, you're on the right track, and the universe will therefore attract whatever you need to fulfil your dream. You can have anything you want, including health, wealth, and happiness—and, by the way, those are the only three things in life that we all actually need, because we can achieve everything else through them.

Health

Have you ever heard of Steven Hawking, one of the finest geniuses and smartest people of the twenty-first century? When he was twenty-one, he was diagnosed with a rare disease called amyotrophic lateral sclerosis (ALS). Doctors told him that he wasn't going to live for more than a couple of years, but look at him now. It's been fifty-three years since then, and boy, doesn't he still look fresh and smart?

See, even though his body is frozen, he has done a lot—not only for us but also for future generations—with his mind-blowing theories like Hawking radiation and countless others. And this proves an important point: even though he has a disability, Steven Hawking has never given up. He fights it, and that's why he has been able to present so many of his wonderful and valuable ideas to the world.

Having a healthy lifestyle is the most important thing of all, and we need to be mindful of its benefits. Scientists say that every human being needs at least thirty minutes of exercise every day, but most people barely do five minutes a week. I might be exaggerating a bit, but you get the point, right?

Sometimes we do manage to exercise, but what do we do afterward? We go to McDonald's and order a Big Mac with fries and a drink, which doesn't make any sense. What you're basically doing is saying, "Oh well. I exercised, so now I deserve to enjoy this kind of food." And all that means is that your workout is now worthless.

Remember how I said that you can get anything through the law of attraction? Well, guess what: by *anything*, I mean good health and even cures for diseases.

If you're reading this book while struggling with a bad disease, sitting in a wheelchair, or going through anything like that, then guess what: you're already cured! You know why? Because, with the law of attraction, you can resist and also beat your conditions.

I believe that you can do it, but here's the thing: Do you really believe that you can do it by yourself? Because you can't have any doubts about it!

Here's the theory: many scientists and researchers believe that the mind controls the body, which means that microbes, viruses, and even diseases can't enter your body or survive there unless you (or your mind) let them.

Terry Fox is a prime example. He was a normal person, just like the rest of us, until the age of nineteen. He was then diagnosed with a rare type of cancer (osteosarcoma), and doctors had no choice but to cut off his right leg. But do you think that he gave up, like many people who have cancer do? No! He fought his cancer. He practiced running and ran five thousand kilometers all across Canada. He started his run with the goal of raising $24.17 million—one dollar for every Canadian. He ran in all kinds of weather and on all kinds of terrain.

The heroic Canadian is gone now, but guess what: his legacy continues. To date, over $650 million has been raised for cancer research, in Terry's name, through the annual Terry Fox Run, held across Canada and around the world. That is why you should continue to fight instead of letting any health issues defeat you. You should take the fight to your disease; don't let your disease take the fight to you.

Remember that the cure is in your mind. Diseases can't last in a body that is controlled by a positive outlook. Medicines are important to fighting illness, but what matters more is your brain's ability to keep your spirits up throughout the healing process. If you believe that you have a healthy body, well, then guess what: your body will get itself back in working order as soon as possible by fighting against any kind of interference. You just have to remember that the disease isn't too strong for you.

We humans all have this limitless power, so we should never let any kind of disease take command of our bodies. We are the rulers of our bodies, and we run them entirely with our positive and powerful approach, thus maintaining full control over any unwelcome, disruptive visitors.

Wealth

In this section, I am going to talk about prosperity and everything comes with it.

When people say that money doesn't grow on trees, or that you have to work hard for your money, what does that mean to you? When you think like that, the universe says, "Your wish is my command," and it becomes more and more difficult to make money or overcome your financial problems.

Now, when our parents see financial experts, what do they typically want from them? Isn't it some helpful tips on how they can generate or save more money? Actually, when you hire a financial expert, he or she will tell you what you already know, suggestions such as, "Don't buy that; it costs too much money" or "You waste your money too fast" or "Don't spend your money without thinking first."

So what I'm trying to say is that you don't need a financial expert to help you generate or save money because that knowledge is in your mind already. If you want to make money, then here's what you have to do: think straight. How do you do that? Well, to start, don't spend lots of money on clothes, online shopping, or even recently released games like *Call of Duty: Black Ops III*. Now that I'm talking about it, I'm getting the shivers. Why would you pay as much as $60 to $120 for a new game? Why would you do that? I never do that, and I don't recommend that you do it either.

What I do recommend, as a sensible option, is what I do all the time. I go to the recycle bin and get an older version of the game, or I wait for that game to get older and then buy it for much less. If you don't like buying used games, then buying new ones on the Internet is simple. You can easily check various websites to find the best deals. And the same goes for clothing. I've seen people buying four-hundred-dollar shoes or caps—that's a lot, man. Why would we pay that much money for that kind of stuff? Maybe it's because we think the quality is better, or maybe most of our friends are wearing branded clothes or shoes, and we don't want to feel embarrassed in front of them.

The reality is that large companies try to make things out to be bigger than they really are, so exaggeration has a huge role in their strategy. But it doesn't matter that they say their products are made with the best materials in the world. What matters is whether or not we really need to overpay for these items most of the time! As the expression says, "believe nothing of what you hear and only half of what you see." That may be overdoing it, but you get the main idea.

I remember this one time when I bought a pair of nice, expensive branded shoes. I was trying to figure out whether they were really any better than other shoes. Now, when I say *good* shoes, I mean Air Jordans from Nike or similar footwear from Under Armour and other companies. I gave it a lot of thought and, in the end, I realized that it's all in your mind. Those businesses just want to make you think their shoes are better. Well, lots of youths have common, reasonably priced clothing or shoes, and they really love them. It all goes back to your mind. When you think unbranded shoes are bad—"Your wish is my command!"—they rip at the first opportunity. But when it comes to branded ones, you say, "Wow, these shoes are really good!" and so—"Your wish is my command!"—they last two years.

Now, let's be clear: I'm not discouraging you from buying *any* branded objects. What I'm trying to say is just buy one, two, or even three fashionable things—but not ten, twenty, or thirty! Don't spend your money on them when you or your family really need to spend that money on something else. Think about it. It's our parents' discretion to decide when spending is needed and when it is not.

By the way, wealth is not all about how much money you have; it's also about your interactions with others—family relationships, inner relationships, and so forth. Let me explain a bit more. Let's say you have a PlayStation 4 but you don't have anyone to play it with or share your time with. You know what? That's not happiness, and wealth without happiness means nothing. Now, imagine that you're a millionaire who has all kinds of materials at hand to help you have fun and enjoy your life. You might be really happy with this scenario, but again, imagine that you don't have a life partner or any good friends to share all that joy with. That's not wealth or happiness; that's more like constant loneliness.

But wealth doesn't include only relationships and money; the definition is broader than that. What it also includes for some people, like me, is knowledge—which, by the way, is an extremely important factor, because if you don't know what you're doing, then how can you expect to achieve your goals and be successful? By *knowledge* I mean an ability with and understanding of some activity or profession that is beneficial to you and maybe even the people around you. For example, I'm not only an author but a chess player and guitarist as well. It's essential for you to know your talents by the time you're a tween, because that knowledge will ultimately lead you toward your goals and, finally, to success.

You have to figure out what you want to do for a living when you're young. Otherwise, when you grow up, you'll have no idea what you're doing. You will be just like every other average person who works morning to night every day, settles for barely making a living, and feels happy because their salaries will be raised by a couple of percentage points next year. Trust me, that is not what you want to do with your life.

Here's a tip: never try to be like the average person, because being average is boring and lame, and it won't get you any success. For example, the average person reads many different kinds of books from science fiction to romance, but wise people tend to read books that actually teach them something valuable, raise their level of knowledge, and adjust their perspective. I'm just saying that if you want to be successful, then don't act like the average person. Do you think that successful people ever act like they're average? No way; not at all. For instance, while everyone else was fooling around, living their average lives, Einstein worked his butt off to be successful, and he got results.

Now, I'm not saying that you should suffer every day, but to benefit from your time wisely, you need to set goals and struggle to reach those goals—that's the way to build yourself an amazing future. As Mohammad Ali, the best boxer of all time, said: "Suffer now and live the rest of your life as a champion."

Happiness

For me, happiness includes living with my parents, being a successful and wealthy businessperson, and owning the newest technologies. But remember, different people have different opinions; therefore, try not to argue with your friends, or anyone else for that matter, over what actually makes someone happy.

To me, happiness stands out from all the other emotions because it's the only one that makes you feel good. It makes you laugh and feel joyful, and it gives you the energy to continue. In fact, happiness is the fuel of humanity; without it, we always sense that something is missing from our lives, and we can't seem to face our daily difficulties. So, whatever it is that makes you unhappy, don't let it get to you. If you want to scream in an empty room or take a walk alone outside—or if you feel the need to do something really silly—then go ahead and do it so you can get that feeling out of you; whether it's sadness, embarrassment, or anger, just don't let it get to you.

But be careful. Don't be too impulsive in your actions, because you might do something really stupid or say something to hurt someone's feelings—like when you tell a joke about someone for fun but he or she happens to be sensitive and gets offended Always try to laugh with others, not at them, because the best way to grow and spread happiness is to share it.

Turn Anger to Motivation

Whether you think you can or you think you can't, you're right.

—Henry Ford

Have you heard of Henry Ford? Do you think his last name might be a bit familiar? The reason for this is that he built some of the first-ever cars and developed the gigantic Ford Motor Company.

Henry Ford (who was born in 1863) dreamed of making machines with wheels on them that could transport people easily from one place to another. When he tried to explain his idea to others, they laughed at him like he was nothing more than a dreamer. But he didn't let other people shatter his dreams; unstoppable to the

41

end, he continued to work on them. He made lots of mistakes along the way, but at least he learned from those mistakes. Finally, in 1908, Ford made the first Model T car, which—since it could be mass-produced— revolutionized the car industry forever. He became one of the most famous people in the United States at the time and also one of the most successful men of the twentieth century.

Ford is a great example of someone who set his goals high and worked to achieve them, which is what you should try to do. Many others followed in his footsteps, including Ferdinand Porsche, Enzo Ferrari, and Ferruccio Lamborghini. Don't these names sound familiar to you? Read them again!

Never let your family problems, or a rough childhood in particular, keep you from following your dreams. Marilyn Monroe was abandoned by her widowed mother, and she spent much of her childhood in foster homes. Bill Clinton was born to a widowed mother and was sent to live with his grandparents as a child. He was later adopted by his mother's second husband, an abusive alcoholic. He was only the second president in US history to have been adopted (Gerald Ford is the other one). John Lennon was adopted by his aunt, when his father left home and his mother was unable to care for him. Steve Jobs was also adopted, at birth, by Paul and Clara Jobs.

Here's another good lesson: never let excuses take control of your mind and discourage you from following your dreams. You can even use those excuses like a turbocharger to propel you toward your dreams. When you're angry and think that the whole world is against you, for instance, just put that anger into setting your goals and working to achieve them. Even when you're stressed and under pressure, you can confront those

feelings in a positive way.

<u>Being Grateful</u>

Here's the deal—if you want something from the law of attraction, then you have to first be grateful for what you already have. So let's say you really want a new game that recently launched in the market. Well, before you can receive it from the law of attraction, you'll have to be grateful for the games that you already have, like *Grand Theft Auto*, *Minecraft,* and *Call of Duty: Black Ops*.

Now, you might say, "Oh, Shervin! That's hard to remember." From time to time, we easily forget to be grateful for what we own or have at hand already, but here's an easy way to remember. What I do is pick a small object—a tiny piece of rock or a doll or anything like that—and every morning when I wake up and see that object beside my bed, it reminds me to be grateful for whatever I have. This is not a joke; it's a very

45

powerful tool to help you reach your dreams. If you're not grateful for whatever you own now—whether it's a game, clothing, or your good health—then you'll have no way to attract more success into your life. Your current situation is the basis for your future, and when you try to be thankful for your current situation, you will then be able to achieve what you envision for the future.

Believe me when I say that we have lots of things to be grateful for, like the water we drink, the beauty of nature all around us, the educational facilities we have at our schools, and so on. Just imagine—some countries don't even have one of those things. That's why we have to be grateful that we live in such a great country like Canada, which gives us the chance and the freedom to be educated so that we can improve and ultimately make the most of ourselves. And that's why I strongly advise you to start using the law of attraction to your advantage

every day. Trust me—it can and will change your life.

More about the Law of Attraction

I will now discuss how the law of attraction works.
Consider the book that you're looking at right now. You
know that it's a physical object, but you don't know how
the paper was made or how the entire book was
manufactured or marketed. Likewise, even though you
watch TV every day, you have no idea how it works or
how the programs are broadcasted or transmitted to your
home—but you benefit from it anyway. It's the same
thing with video games: you don't know how the gaming
console reads the disc or how pressing a certain button
causes the video game to take a certain action.

Now, you might say, "Shervin, we can read the
book, we can watch the TV, and we can play the game.
We know that they exist, because we have proof. But we
don't have any proof that the law of attraction exists."
Well, let me answer your question like this: Do we

actually see the electricity when it comes into a lamp? No, we only use its energy to turn the lamp on; we don't care how it works. What about the law of gravity? Do we really see it in action? No, but it works too. The same is true for the law of motion.

Now, ask yourself this question: How badly do you want to change your life? If you still doubt your ability to succeed, then try this exercise. I want you to set a really high but reasonably attainable goal that will make your mind explode if you reach it. After that, follow the steps that I've presented in this book. When you finally do achieve your goal, trust me, you will be amazed.

At this point, I would like to mention something important that can really affect your progress toward success. I'm referring to the difference between the things you want and the things you don't want. Let me ask you a simple question. Let's say somebody shows you a cup of milk that is both half-full and half-empty. If you wanted to describe the cup, would you say that it was half-full or half-empty?

If you would look at the cup and say that it's half-full, then you're a positive person. On the other hand, if you would focus on the cup's being half-empty, then you might be a little bit more negative. So many people see the empty half of the cup, but they don't see how they should be grateful for the half they do have, because they could have easily not even had that. If you're one of the people who sees the half-full cup, then that's great news, as you are already thankful for whatever you currently have.

I don't know whether you've realized this fact or not, but in life, the more you give, the more you get. And the more grateful you are, the more you achieve. Now, if you actually want a full cup of milk—or an Xbox or anything else that you've been looking for—then ask for it in the right way. Saying, "I really want to find a good friend," is a positive way to ask for what you want; complaining, "I'm really alone; can't I find any friends?" is not. Avoid asking for things in a negative way!

See, when you think bad thoughts, they always become reality. But when you think good ones, they are more likely to come true too. In this way, whether you like it or not, your actions, emotions, and thoughts are what cause various things to happen, so you have to direct them correctly. If you wanted to get an *A* in math, you could say, "I don't want anything like a *B* or a *C*." If you say it like that, though, guess what: you'll keep on getting *B*s and *C*s. So be careful how you ask the law of attraction for what you want.

The Steps of the Law of Attraction

Now, when you think something like "I want a job," but then you just sit there doing nothing to find one, it doesn't work at all. You're all like, "Duh!" Well, guess what—you do this every day!

You have to take certain steps, and then the law of attraction will step in; it will not help you if you just sit there doing nothing. As for me, if I said, "I am going to write a book" but did nothing to help myself—well, that wouldn't do jack. You have to take actions to move yourself forward. Don't allow life to control you; you have to take control of your life.

I'm going to tell you the three steps of the law of attraction, but first I have to tell you something fairly significant: *decide what you really want.* What's the one thing that you want intensely? What is the one thing that you believe you deserve? Write it down on a piece of paper (note that it needs to be something realistic) and then complete the following steps:

1. Imagine

What do you really want? Is it good grades? Do you want to be the most athletic person in your school or maybe one of the best performers in your school's band? You've got to focus on that one thing you want, whether it's an impressive body with a six-pack or better marks. Just write it down and imagine it coming true.

The power of the brain is incredible, but we humans usually use only a percentage of it. A huge amount of our mental capacity is always left unused, and we can use a little bit of it to get to our goal.

The power of human imagination is so intense—it's beyond anyone's imagination! You can basically visualize everything in your head, and if your imagination is strong, you can even sense the things that you envision. In fact, when you imagine something, it's like you're in another dimension.

Don't be that person who thinks imagination is only for young children. No, no, no—do not make that mistake! Imagination is for all humans, and it helps us to reach our dreams. Without it, we would never have the world that we do now. All the progress that we've made over thousands of years is due to imagination. So, basically, the law of attraction attracts everything that you can possibly imagine in your brain. And by *everything*, I mean everything.

2. Believe It's Possible

After you've imagined whatever you want most, you have to take the second step of the law of attraction: you have to believe it's possible. For instance, let's say that I want to get really great marks in school by the end of the year or win that school competition. So I start to imagine it, and then I have to believe in it. I need to believe that I have already reached my goal and see myself in that situation. I'm not talking about a fake visualization but a real event that will result in your believing in yourself, which will in turn increase your self-confidence so that you can achieve your dream. When you're trying to attract something, you have to act like a winner who has already reached his or her goal. So don't forget—act like a winner, be a winner.

Believing that it's possible to attract something you want also allows you to better understand *how* to attract it. Say that you want to be a soccer player, so you imagine and believe that you're a soccer player on a daily basis. This helps you to think of the many ways you can become one. For example, the first thing to do is lose some weight, because in soccer, you have to be fit so that you can run rapidly for ninety minutes. The second thing to do is practice. If you want to achieve your goal, then you have to practice achieving it over and over again. So take action, and then wait for the great result to come.

As I mentioned before, Muhammad Ali once said, "Don't quit. Suffer now and live the rest of your life as a champion." Again, I'm not saying that you should suffer all the time, but you should definitely work hard in order to achieve your goals. Want good marks? You need to imagine and believe that you have good marks, but, at the same time, you can't just sit there and do nothing to better them. You need to study, stay focused, listen well in class, and do your homework consistently. Only then will you believe that you've learned well enough to be ready for the exam.

3. Receive

When you reach the third step, you are finally ready to achieve your goal and receive your reward. This comes after all the hard work that you've done as a result of using your imagination. You were able to see what you wanted most in your mind and then started to believe that you already had it. You established the goal that you hoped to accomplish, and then you worked intensely toward that goal without ever giving up. Now you can celebrate your victory and see that the sacrifices you had to make were worth it—and by sacrifices, I mean half an hour less of TV time or something like that, which is a really small sacrifice compared to your enormous success.

This is the time for you to be proud of yourself for what you have done. And now, you can do the same for any goal that comes to mind. Of course, this doesn't mean that your journey with the law of attraction is over. You can start imagining, believing, and receiving as soon as you have achieved your first goal!

Thinking Differently

In this world, the people who think outside of the box are the only ones likely to succeed, because they look at reality differently. And the people who think differently—or even in a weird way—are typically winners because they avoid routine and cliché, which makes their ideas fresh. So, if you want to be successful in life, always try to think differently. Let's look at Walk Disney's story, for instance.

<u>Walt Disney</u>

Walt Disney, who was born in 1901, was a man of unique vision. At a very young age, he became interested in drawing, so in high school, he took his drawing lessons seriously. Note that when you have a lightbulb above

59

your head, you should never let it go—that's one part of the law of attraction.

When he was ready, Disney started a company called Laugh-O-Gram Studio, but that was a complete failure as the company went bankrupt. Still, the most important thing to take away from this is that he didn't quit. In fact, he soon started to build another business and made his famous Alice comedies, for which he got recognized as a Hollywood figure. In 1932, Disney released the first color cartoon, *Flowers and Trees*, which was pretty funny for its time. Near the end of 1937, he released his first full-length movie, *Snow White and the Seven Dwarfs*. After that, he went on to create *Dumbo, Pinocchio, Fantasia, Bambi*, and many more.

You can see how Walt Disney looked at the world differently, and that's what you have to do in order to be successful—you have to look at the world from a different perspective than other people. He was the first person to make animated cartoons and realize that you can sell associated merchandise. The same goes for Henry Ford: when everyone else was riding horses and using roller skates, he was hard at work designing a mechanical machine that could take you anywhere.

Anyone who has achieved such success first had a different vision or, more specifically, thought outside of the box. That's how you should think—and then act on it! If you have a new idea or point of view, then say it out loud, without any doubt. Let's say that you have some unusual ideas while you're at school (or anywhere else). Well, no matter whether the people around you might think they're stupid or weird, you just have to explain those ideas, and I promise that it will benefit you in a huge way.

Let me share a personal experience with you that has to do with having a different vision. One day, I was with my parents, shopping at a big grocery store. I noticed a photographer, who had many cameras and other equipment, taking pictures of the boxes on the shelves from different perspectives. They were all simple boxes that most people wouldn't even have noticed, but this photographer seemed really serious. The lesson here is that he was looking for something that no one else could see. This is what you have to do—you have to look at the world in a way that other people won't.

Always ask yourself, "What am I doing?" and then, "What is the purpose of doing it?" When you have the answers, determine whether the purpose and outcome of what you're doing are worthwhile. Always do this before doing anything important, because you should always know and believe in the purpose of your actions.

Otherwise, you'll face a lot of disappointment and regret.

Change

Change is part of our world. Everything around us changes on a daily basis, and so nothing in our environment remains the same for long. Change is an important factor in all of our lives as it can assist us in finding a better way to meet our goals. Now, changes are either good or bad; it is your responsibility to choose between them.

So what's a good change? Well, when your marks have gone from a *C+* to an *A*, that is a really good change—and a big achievement. Your marks falling from a *C+* to an *F*, however, would be a bad change. It is your job to direct such changes, but you have to be careful when you do, because your life could easily change for the worse. You might become bankrupt or even lose the ones you love, but that is entirely up to you.

Are you a positive person or a negative person? Again, as I have said over a thousand times, negativity brings you nothing but misery. But who knows? You might still turn out to be a successful businessperson or university professor, or a famous actor or dancer. Just make sure to continue down a good track. Don't ever quit, and be positive. If you had told me three years ago that I was going to learn this much English and French in this amount of time, I would have laughed in your face. Well, let me tell you this: "No dream is too big and no dreamer too small."

The most important factor in finding any kind of success is thinking big. Let me demonstrate. When I first set a goal to learn English, I thought, "I can't do this." Well, guess what: "Your wish is my command." Always remember that nothing is impossible—you just have to believe that you can do it, take action, and move forward.

So don't worry about the possibility of not reaching your

goal. When I first started to write this book, I had my

doubts; I felt like it couldn't compete with other, really

popular books. But, according to the rules of the law of

attraction, you can never doubt your abilities. And

remember, "Our doubts are traitors."

<u>Fear</u>

Fear is one of the most powerful emotions—and it could be the worst one of all. Sometimes, feeling afraid is good and even necessary, because that's what tells you not to jump from a ten-story building. Even so, you have to be able to control the level of fear in your mind so that it supports rather than stops your progress toward success.

Now, when I started writing this book, I felt afraid. I wondered whether it was going to be taken seriously. And what about readers' reactions to it? What if it was a failure? The worst thing you can do is doubt or dread what you are doing. Those feelings will only cause you to fail over and over again, so put them away completely. Don't be afraid of failure, because you'll find success only when you defeat your fears.

As Mark Zuckerberg, the founder of Facebook, said, "The biggest risk is not taking any risk." What he's trying to tell us is that sometimes we have to overcome our fear and take a feasible risk in order to be successful. Remember that the risks must be reasonable and the goals achievable. Let's say, for instance, that whenever your teacher asks the class a question, you're always the one who sits still and keeps your hand down, too afraid to answer it. One day, take the risk and raise your hand! It's a small step but in the right direction. You've got nothing to lose—either your answer is correct or it's not, and then you sit back down. Sometimes even little risks can make a big difference. Just give it a shot!

This might seem like a really simple example to you, but think about it: it's always the little risks and small steps that help us continue on to the bigger ones. Mark Zuckerberg took big risks. If you had told him in the beginning that 1.5 billion people would use his website and that he would become a billionaire, he probably would have laughed in your face and said that it was just a small idea. Well, guess what: small ideas are the ones that most often change the world.

So what I'm trying to say is that nothing happens by accident or chance, but everything happens for a reason. Even a simple, small idea that comes to your mind might lead you to a big achievement that nobody could have never imagined, and it might just change people's lives for the better. Now, think about it: Was it an accident that a meteor hit the Earth and wiped out the dinosaurs? Was it an accident that you bought this book or decided to read it now?

Follow Your Dreams

One of the worst things that fear can do is make you doubt yourself and keep you from following your dreams. When you doubt your dreams, you will never be able to follow them to success. If you don't have any dreams, then you don't have any goals for your life—and in today's world, if you are living without goals, then your life is all about survival. Don't worry about how impossible you believe your goal may be; you have to believe in yourself no matter what. That's the important part—just meet your goal and make your dreams come true.

Now, you might have one person in your life who will always keep you from following your dreams. Do you often find yourself saying, "he won't let me" or "she won't let me"? As I said at the beginning of this book, take complete responsibility for your life—not anyone else's, yours. Blaming other people for your problems is a poor excuse for being too lazy to follow your dreams, and if you let other people take responsibility for your life, then who knows what awful things may happen?

But try not to be too enthusiastic at the start, because it's really difficult to set a goal and then have the limitless determination necessary to meet it. You should be passionate about what you're doing in the first couple of weeks—when you're all, "Woo-hoo! Let's do this!"—but then, weeks later—when you feel like saying, "Oh my God, this is so freaking exhausting" or "I'm not going to do this anymore"—you still have to feel that same level of excitement. You also have to be able and willing to make sacrifices to achieve your goals. I don't mean that you have to make big sacrifices. You can go without things like TV time or game time, for instance, if that will give you the time and energy you need to pursue your dreams. It's all about give and take. Give it your all and you will definitely receive a valuable benefit in return.

Remember, when we achieve our goals, our self-confidence gets a big boost, like from a rocket. We all have only one life, so make sure that you live yours amazingly well.

It's the truth that when you grow up, you want to see a past that you're proud of, not a past full of regrets. You don't want to look back and see how you wasted your life on something that wasn't really important, let alone beneficial. If you just watch TV or useless YouTube videos or play video games all day, do you think that you'll be able to change your life? I'm not saying that I don't do these things at all—we all need to have fun and play—but think about it. Sometimes some of us become virtually addicted to them.

When you believe in a dream and invest your time and dedication into meeting it, well, guess what: "Your wish is my command." The law of attraction will find the easiest and fastest way to get you to that dream. But remember, the law of attraction will either find the easiest and fastest way to make your life better or find the easiest and fastest way to make your life miserable—in any case, you're in control.

<u>Creating a Vision Board</u>

Here, I would like to recommend a really great tool that you can use to keep track of your dreams: the vision board. This amazingly simple idea has worked for many people on their journey to success.

So what is a vision board? It's a board that showcases your goals in pictures or various papers that you glue or staple to it. It could include an inspirational picture relevant to your dream or a note reminding you of what you hope to accomplish—anything that will remind you of your mission can be on your vision board.

What's the purpose of a vision board, you ask? Well, just imagine visualizing all your dreams every night before you go to sleep and again in the morning when you wake up. By doing this over and over, you help your mind to align itself with your goals. In this way, you can use a vision board as an unbelievably powerful tool

to inspire your dedication on your own wonderful

journey.

<u>Inner Peace</u>

From the beginning of your life and throughout it, the only person you can truly rely on is yourself, so you need to make sure that you're completely at peace with yourself.

Believe me, everyone goes through a number of stressful periods in their lifetime. There will come a time when you feel like you're full of stress or under some kind of pressure, and you'll badly want to be alone—just imagine it! Say that you're the person who's always being picked on at school or the target of trash talk among your friends. You feel like you have the pressure of a thousand pounds on you. You ask yourself why the whole world is against you, and you think that something might be wrong with you.

First of all, if you think that you're a really hopeless and uncool person or that nobody at school likes you, and even if your classmates don't treat you as well as they do the other kids—don't underestimate yourself! And second of all, never think that you don't have the ability to engage with others. In fact, you need to realize that the so-called cool kids at your school are not all that special.

Actually, no one is special—everybody just uses his or her capabilities to develop and eventually become successful. That's why there is always such a difference between people like businesspeople, who make millions of dollars per year just by selling ordinary things, and most of the people living paycheck to paycheck, who are working ordinary jobs. Lots of people don't take any risks and stick with what they know for a long period of time. Others do take risks and remain open to opportunities for positive change; these are the people who will attract the most success in their lifetimes.

This is why we seriously need to think big when it comes to the future, especially while we're still young. We have to be self-starters so that we can take control of our own destiny and push on toward our dreams. You might notice some of the "cool" guys at school—the ones who have a great sense of humor. They're popular because they make people laugh, but they have only two roads in front of them: they can choose to use their talents and popularity to serve their development—they may even become very popular stand-up comedians or movie stars someday—or they can simply do nothing to help themselves follow their dreams, not even taking any relevant classes. Wasting your time while waiting for a miracle to happen will never bring you any prosperity or happiness. And guess what: miracles don't happen in real life. Always remember that we all have only two roads to choose from, and we are the only ones who can make that choice.

One of the things that keeps us from finding inner peace is thinking too much about our daily problems, which are often really small or even stupid. The human brain has the ability to make things seem either bigger or smaller in our minds. This means that we can make every little problem into a big one or, conversely, make a gigantic problem smaller and easier to deal with than it really is. Again, everything depends on our ability to control our brain. Imagine that you want to buy a pair of Nike shoes but, due to a financial problem, you can't. And you may feel some peer pressure because you think that literally everybody else has those shoes and you're the only one with a much less attractive brand. Well, stop worrying about this stupid problem. You're wasting your brainpower on that when you have way more important things to worry about. You're thinking, "If I don't get those Nike shoes, then people will judge me badly." But you never stop to imagine that those people might not even care!

So don't pay attention to other people's judgments and just go with whatever you believe is right. It's not as if I'm forcing you to not buy those things; you can go and buy as many shoes as you want, but remember, nothing is worth it if you're being forced to do something that you don't want to do. One time, I recall that I had a severe case of peer pressure over my clothing styles and the way I might look at school. But when I thought about it again, I instantly told myself, "Who cares if people judge me as long as I'm happy with what I'm doing or wearing and it makes me feel good or comfortable." Different people have different perspectives. One person might say that your schoolbag is great while another one might say that it's too small or old-fashioned. The same sort of thing can apply to your hairstyle or overall appearance, but it doesn't matter as long as you have your own perspective and know to respect other people's opinions.

One of the most important things that humans should learn is that sometimes you really have nothing to prove. Clearly, there's no reason for you to feel pressured by your peers, but it's become commonplace—and you think that if you don't go along with what your friends want, you'll feel insecure. Now, this time, actually consider what I'm saying: What's the worst thing that will happen if you don't respond to peer pressure? Nothing will happen! Even when you know you're right, you may feel the need to respond to peer pressure, but believe me, it's best if you don't respond to it at all.

What you need to know when it comes to peer pressure is that, most of the time, it's the person doing the pressuring who feels insecure. That's why it's very important to never argue with the people who do want to spend $500 on shoes or clothes. Do not pit your perspective against theirs; such conversations will get you nowhere, so at the end of the day, they're not really worth having. That said, while you should always respect other people's perspectives, make sure to choose the one that you're OK with.

Now, remember that words may well be the most powerful weapon in the universe when you know how to use them properly. So you have to stop feeling sorry for yourself and worrying all the time. Stop asking yourself questions like, "Will it be bad if I get an *F* this term?" and "Is it bad to not buy a Mother's Day card for my mom?" Whenever you feel really bad and don't know what to do to feel better, think to yourself that a million other situations are far worse than the one you're in. After that, evaluate the situation—stay focused, take your time, and try to come up with some promising ideas that may help you solve your problem.

When I came to Canada, I thought, "Wow, this place is a paradise!" And when I took my first step into my new school, I was like, "This is magnificent—like heaven, or even beyond heaven." When you live in Canada, or any other country like it, you have lots of tools to help raise yourself up and even tons of opportunities to shine. In other words, you have nothing to be negative or worry about.

Now, I would like to share some points with you that will not only help make your life easier as you confront certain challenges but also help you to achieve inner peace more frequently.

Just Deal with It

Don't be too concerned with acne or bullies; those are only the little things in life that you can manage yourself. And you don't have to worry about the bigger things— like war or world hunger—either, because you can't do anything to "stop" them other than make donations and participate in community activities. This is just the nature of life, and you have to deal with it.

Millions of people died in the world wars. My point is that you need to stop concerning yourself with things you can't change. If you don't accept this, and you just keep on worrying, then you'll upset your inner peace. When something is out of your hands, you have zero control over it, so there is no point in being concerned with it or blaming yourself for it.

Spending Time in Nature

Spending time in nature is a great way to get your mind off your troubles and really focus on the beauty that the world has to offer, like its beautiful blue seas, tall green trees, and magnificent mountain ranges. So take a walk or ride a bike outside. That's where our ancestors lived, and besides, it helps to develop inner your peace.

You don't necessarily need to go outside to enjoy nature. You can also appreciate it from home by watching a documentary or reading your favorite book in front of a window, or on your balcony so that you can admire the scenery. Spending time in nature is also a really good opportunity for everyone to put their electronic devices down and discover what it feels like to be a caveman.

<u>Laughter</u>

If you were to ask my classmates what I love to do, they would most likely tell you that I love to laugh and make others laugh.

The moment you start smiling or laughing, the world becomes a much better place to live, not only for you but for everyone else around you as well. It's like a magic trick that every person knows but rarely uses. If you're under a lot of stress that you shouldn't even have at your age, then use laughter to change your mood for the better. Scientific studies have shown that laughter can drastically decrease stress hormones in the brain. So whenever something bad happens to you and you feel an emotion—maybe it's anger or disgust or any other negative feeling—try to reduce and ultimately control it with a little bit of laughter. Smile at the world, and the world will smile back at you.

Let's say you wake up in the morning and fall out of bed. You say, "Crap, why did this happen to me? It's my bad luck. Life sucks!" You're only attracting negative thoughts along with bad feelings. Now, say you leave your home to go to school. You've already attracted negative thoughts, so what happens next? Suddenly, it starts to rain. You say, "Oh, see! I knew it—my life sucks." All of these outbursts come from negativity. Next, at your after-school soccer game, you slip on the ball; you don't only hurt yourself but someone else too.

Now, let's consider another scenario where you wake up and fall from the bed but you laugh about it and keep yourself in a positive mood. After that, it starts to rain outside and you don't have an umbrella, but you know what—who cares? It's not a big deal at all! When this happens to us, we may even want to try running in the rain. Have you ever tried that before, just for fun? It could be a really unforgettable experience, and you're going to have lots of fun, believe me! Anyway, if you have a soccer game after school, and you slip on the ball and happen to hit another player, you can just say "sorry" to your friend and then you can both laugh about it. You may feel a little bit of pain at first, but with a positive attitude and a smile, things won't seem so bad!

Always remind yourself that the universe treats us the same way we treat it.

<u>Never Lose Hope</u>

Never ever lose hope.

This is a lesson that everybody has to learn as fast and as soon as possible. Hope is so important that if you lose it, your life falls apart. Similarly, if even only some of the team members lose hope in a soccer match, then the whole team fails. So whenever you feel like you're losing hope, delete that thought from your mind, and get up or try again. Humans have the capability to restart over and over again, and every time we do, we have more experience from the previous loss. So we need to take these lessons, learn not to repeat our mistakes, and move forward.

Hope is also a path to peace and success. If I lose hope in writing this book and struggle with bad thoughts—like, "What if this book doesn't get finished?"

or "What if it isn't received well by readers?" or "What if it isn't good enough to publish?"—then the whole work will go away.

Alexander Graham Bell failed 257 times before he finally found the right frequency to make the telephone. Wow! 257 times—can you believe it? Personally, if I fail to make anything only three times, I sometimes feel like quitting. But, seriously, look at this man's determination! He never gave up or lost hope, not even on the one hundredth or two hundredth try. And that is why we have smartphones in our pockets right now. Isn't this a massive lesson for every single one of us? Bell himself might have wanted to transfer this important message to you: you should never ever lose your hope. You should always give it another try, no matter what *it* is, and you will always ultimately win.

Also, embrace your dreams, and let no one crush them. If I were to tell my classmates that I'm writing a book, they would probably laugh at me and say, "Yeah, right." But don't let anyone crush your dreams. As soon as you let that happen, you lose hope. When you lose hope, you think bad thoughts. And when you think bad thoughts, you start to worry. Finally, when you worry too much, you give up on your beliefs and motivation.

You know, they say that, according to the laws of physics, it's impossible for a bee to fly because its wings are too small to carry its relatively heavy body. But the bees don't care what those laws say. They fly by instinct anyway. What this tells you is that you don't have to care what other people say or think; you only have to be careful that your words and thoughts are right and let no one else's words affect you. Besides, all people have their own perspective, but no one else has your perspective. If you follow other people's views, then your life will fall apart—you won't have inner peace, and you won't find success.

Nobody's Perfect

If you don't have all the answers, that's fine. Nobody knows everything. Stick with what you do know and keep on learning more and more about whatever interests you. Nobody wants you to understand quantum physics—and if you don't know what that means, it's fine.

I personally believe that we have yet to learn everything, and every day is a new opportunity to develop. All the information that I have learned so far is from various sources, which include my parents, a variety of books and articles, and (most importantly) today's best teacher—the Internet. Everybody needs to keep pushing to increase their level of knowledge, especially in their fields of interest. No successful person ever knew everything from day one; all of them had to learn along the way, and then, little by little, they made their success.

So it's very important that you don't focus on your

weaknesses but stick to your strengths. If you do this,

then your weak points will toughen up and ultimately

become strong points.

<u>Live in the Present</u>

Don't worry about the past or the future. And don't worry about the things you can't change; just live in the present and go with the flow. Of course, you can always think about what you're going to do next. Keep on going forward, and never stop. Also, try to have fun with every second of your life, because one day, when you're older, you will have all these adventurous memories.

Now, focus on this moment, the one in which you're reading this book. Are you getting anywhere by reading it? How are you feeling right now?

How to Face Tween's Common Problems

Bullying

I believe that all of us have been bullied at least once or twice in our lives, or maybe even every day. Verbal bullying is one type of bullying. Sure, they say, "Sticks and stones may break my bones, but words will never hurt me." But, guess what! Whoever first said that was wrong. After all, words are the most powerful weapons in the universe.

Words do hurt you, badly, so here are some ways you can stop that from happening. But be careful, because there is a huge difference between teasing and bullying. If a person is teasing you, then it's just for fun, and you generally laugh along with them. But if the person is bullying you, then they're doing it to hurt you on purpose. The only reason a bully will bully you is to hurt your feelings—and you're just the kind of person that he or she likes to pick on.

When you're being bullied, you can't cry, you can't get emotional, and you can't run away. Don't even tell the teacher, or any other person in charge, until it gets serious. When you combine your brain and careful words, you get a beautiful combination. That's the only way to defeat a verbal bully without actually bullying them yourself. For instance, once a bully came up to me and said, "You're ugly." So what did I say? I said, "Thank you. I've been working on it, and now my face is banned in thirteen different states, so if I step inside the border, they nuke me." The bully walked away as if I was crazy.

If a person comments on you once, you say, "Stop." If the person does it again, you say, "Stop," but in a strong, serious manner, and then you add, "or I'm going to tell the teacher." And if it happens a third time, then you tell the teacher right away. Remember, you don't want to take bullies too seriously, because—trust me—they're not going to make a living out of this. Treat them as if they're a joke and they will stop picking on you—remember what the law of attraction says: "Your wish is my command." To answer the verbal bully, you can make your own combination of words in your brain. But it has to be something that won't insult the other person. One time, someone insulted me and I said, "If you say so." He was like, "Aren't you insulted?" So then I said, "That's what they all say." These two sentences are the perfect combination to screw a bully up.

Now, remember: talking back is not insulting. Sometimes you may want to accept what they're telling you, if it's not serious. Right now you're thinking, "Accept it? Accept what?" You accept what the bully tells you, like that you're ugly. "Well, OK! I'm ugly!" It can't possibly hurt you as long as you know that you're really beautiful, and besides, you've literally burned the bully. No one can respond to this kind of acceptance, and so, there's nothing but an awkward silence afterward. The bully, knowing that the fight is lost, might say that you're weird before walking away, and then you can do your victory dance. If that doesn't work, use the teacher as a last resort.

Always know that a bully wants to fight you. So don't fight the bully—that will only cause you more trouble. Oh, and here comes another lesson: don't answer bullying with bullying. If you answer bullying with bullying, then you're no better than the bully. It's like executing a serial killer; if you kill that person, then you're no better. One of the most important lessons in the world is that muscles don't matter, but brains do! If a bully has big muscles, it doesn't mean that he's smart. In fact, all of his muscles are so big that his brain can't fit inside his body and you can easily outsmart him.

I have one last truly important thing to tell you. When you get bullied, you get offended. And who tells you that you're offended? Your brain! You've trained your brain to be easily offended, and so you react impulsively. But you can take care of yourself by training your brain to handle pressure.

<u>Cyberbullying</u>

When technology came into our lives and we got advanced online games and social media networks, a new problem emerged: cyberbullying. It's basically verbal bullying on the Internet.

So what do you do when you get cyberbullied? Here are some things you can do. Do not respond, except to type *stop*, because the moment you respond, the bully achieves his or her goals. Besides, if you respond, you're only letting your anger out. When you say "stop" and the person doesn't stop, you save the evidence, and you block that person. If you realize this is happening over and over, then ask a trusted adult to report it to the police for investigation. Make sure that you always get some help from your parents or teachers, because cyberspace is a place where bullies can get away fast. If the cyberbully is posting really violent comments or doing any kind of criminal activity—like posting pictures without your permission—then you absolutely have to inform an adult and get help from law enforcement. One last thing: make sure that you're always civil on the Internet so that you don't easily become a bully's target.

We're about done with the bullying chapter, but I wanted to say one last thing to the bullies who are reading this book. I want to remind you that it's seriously not cool to pick on people who aren't your size—or even people who are your size. I know that something has happened to you in your lifetime to make you feel frustrated or angry, but you can't take it out on other people. If you continue to do this, who knows what will become of you. So please reconsider your behavior—seriously—and remember that it's never too late to change. What I invite you to do is apologize to every person you have ever bullied and ask for everyone's forgiveness. Trust me, this will change your life in a big way.

<u>Reality</u>

When you become an adult, you finally have to face reality—telling you now is better than forcing you to figure it all out later. But seriously, talk to your parents about this.

When we go out into the real world, we will be faced with a much tougher reality than we know now. There might even be some savage wolves out there who will see most people as sheep and be willing to abuse our simplicity and kindness in particular. So it's up to us to be better prepared and smarter than they are. Now, I'm telling you this so that you don't think you'll always be this age. I know that being a preteen or tween rocks, but everybody grows both physically and mentally. I'm telling you this so that, as you grow up, you can make plans for your life—and a life without a calendar is trash.

Remember when I said that you shouldn't live like the average person? Well, here's another reason for that. To the average person, living a successful life is very difficult—it involves working at a franchise, buying expensive stuff, and not taking any risks. I'm not saying that working is bad; working is really good, but working for someone else when you don't have any goals for the whole rest of your life is not a good idea. You can always start your own business in your own specialty and follow your own life path. It doesn't matter whether that business is small or big, as long as it's yours. When you grow up, you can make your own destiny and take control of it. In this way, you will have passed the reality test and succeeded in life.

Reality presents us with a lot of opportunities and prospects, but what's critical is how we face it—and remember, everybody has to face it sooner or later, so we need to prepare ourselves for a better future by setting a certain goal and life path in our youth. Most people can't face reality properly. Most of the time, doing so involves lots of frustration and uncertainty. But that's what success is—surviving reality and trying to make the best of it.

Parent Appreciation

The next common preteen problem is not knowing how to show appreciation and love for one's parents. When you're a tween, you usually aren't all that eager to talk to your parents or other grownups a lot, especially in terms of your emotions. But you do have to rely on your parents, and they really can help you by sharing their life experience.

I'm not going to lie—I learned 90 percent of what I know from my parents. You have to trust your parents because they have way more experience than you do. It also needs to be said that our parents have to trust us in return. So how do you gain their trust? Just show them some appreciation. Here are some ways you can show that you love, appreciate, and support your parents:

- **Don't Make Them Ask You Something Twice**

  Parents hate it when you make them ask you to do something twice. Most of the time, I try to do what my parents ask me to, but sometimes I can't get off the couch or stop watching TV. If you're like me in this way, then you have to try harder. You don't want to make anyone outside of your family ask you to do something twice either. As a matter of fact, you should always be the first one to do anything, because that's how leaders are formed in life. You should always want to be the first in the talent that you have.

- **Write a Letter**

  It's a really good thing to let your parents know that you love them in a letter. You could put it under one of their pillows or beside one of their bookmarks. When you do this, your parents will realize that you love them with all of your heart, because they'll see that you took the time to write them a letter, and it actually did take time.

- **Spend Time with Them**

Spending time with your parents is really important; not only will you get to know them a little better, but they will get to know you too. It will also make your social skills way better—no, seriously, it will! And you can do so many different things together. For example, you can spend time together at a movie or while playing or watching a sport. Now, this one might sound crazy, but you should try playing video games with them sometimes. They love playing video games, even though they act like they don't. Give it a shot—you won't be disappointed! And besides, if you play video games with them when they have the time, then you're hitting two targets with one arrow: you're playing a game, and you're spending time with your parents. See? Two objectives achieved.

<u>Constant Need to Look Good</u>

Tweens and preteens always want to look good. It's not that big a deal with boys, but for girls—oh my God!

Boys focus more on hairstyle while girls focus more on—everything. Girls are more aware of their appearance and sensitive to the ways that others might judge them. I'm not saying it's a good thing, and I'm not saying it's a bad thing either. I think that it might not be wise to always be concerned with being good-looking. And I don't really care about looking good all the time. At school, I would rather wear a T-shirt and comfy pants than blue jeans and a sweater that matches the color of my socks.

One of the reasons I think people are obsessed with being good-looking is that they are afraid of being judged. Don't worry, you're beautiful—just the way you are. I'm sure we all know who Albert Einstein was. He had a crazy hairstyle—it looked like he had been struck by lightning. But he's one of the greatest physicists that has ever lived. He had only a few types of shirts and shoes—why? He said that he didn't waste brainpower on little and stupid things. The same thing is true of Mark Zuckerberg. You always see him with his simple gray T-shirt. If you can't handle people judging you, then you can't really be successful.

<u>Electronics</u>

Electronics cause some of the worst problems for tweens and preteens. They're a huge distraction in everyday life, and they can distract you from finding overall success. Video games, for instance, are not only distracting but also addicting, and when you get addicted to them, you can't easily get over it. The way I think you can keep this from happening is by making a schedule for your day so that you won't spend all your time on games. But you have to be committed to your schedule; otherwise, it's not a schedule.

Social Networks

Social networks are the mother of all distractions, and these are the three biggest ones: Facebook, Twitter, and Instagram. So, I'm just going to ask you this question: What are you actually trying to accomplish with social media?

If you're trying to have fun or engage with your friends, well, then there are lots of other ways to do that. You can have fun with your friends when you're playing a board game or doing your homework together. Again, the amount of time you spend on social media needs to be managed and reviewed. Really, everything depends on time management, because it seems that the amount of time that we allocate to these social-media sites is sometimes more that it should be. We need to seriously reduce some of our environmental distractions in order to improve our concentration so that we can focus on our goals.

Have you ever noticed that people who lived one hundred to two hundred years before us—people like Albert Einstein, Thomas Edison, or Isaac Newton—were so successful *despite* having less technology and fewer tools at hand? Do you know why that is? One reason is that they had fewer distractions back then (such as computers, TVs, and video games), so they were able to work hard, with higher concentration. They were also able to manage their time and therefore their lives better, which allowed them to achieve their goals.

We too can achieve our goals if we learn to use the Internet in the right way. Sharing good information with others or regularly visiting informative websites would be really beneficial to us. There are tons of amazing and useful pages on these sites, so go for it and use them. If you want to have a successful life, then you also have to manage social media so that it serves you better. For instance, it can help you to put your goals in perspective as you start looking toward the future. If you want to achieve big, then act big. The Internet and social media are really powerful tools, and they're accessible to almost everyone in today's world. So you've got to start using them now. Everything starts now—believe me!

Academic Pressure

Academic pressure comes from the need or desire to perform well in school and is another common cause of stress. You might think it's a good thing or you might think it's a bad thing—it depends on what type of person you are. In any case, you must remain in control of yourself and not let the academic pressure take over. Here are some ways that you can reduce the stress in your life:

- If you find that your homework or a quiz is really difficult, then break it down into smaller parts.

- Nobody says you're Albert Einstein—just study until you know you're ready for your exam.

- When you're stressed, you need to stay positive; remember that the law of attraction says, "Your wish is my command."

- This might sound odd, but eating may help with your anxiety. Eat the natural vitamins and iron found in good food like fruits and vegetables—these can help you when you're studying under pressure. If those don't help, then you can turn to Burger King or McDonald's. (Just kidding!)

- The day before a test, if you want to, you can study with a friend. Just make sure that your friend is not a negative person who says, "Oh no, we can't do this!" or "We will fail." When he or she is negative like that, the law of attraction says, "Your wish is my command."

- When a friend asks you to come over for a party or a birthday dinner the night before a test, don't be afraid to say no. Saying no is one of the things you have to master in life, and saying no will also build up your confidence.

Now, you've done everything on the list and you're about to take a test. Stay calm and breathe deeply, because as soon as you're not calm, you freak out, and when you freak out, you lose control. Some scientists say that chewing gum while taking a test improves your grade; I don't know if that's true, but if you want to, you can give it a try. Strategically, just focus on the test and look for clues that will help you find the solutions. Don't say that there aren't any—there is always a clue and there is always a solution.

Not Having Friends

For most of us, not having friends feels like a massive problem. Some people think that they don't have friends, but they actually know tons of people who support them.

You may get upset and say that nobody likes you, but what you don't understand is that you just don't know how to make friends. Making friends can be easy—you just have to follow my tactics. So, if you're under the illusion that you're alone and have no friends, please don't think that way. You're not alone, and you potentially have lots of friends.

Being social is really important if you want to successfully make friends. So how do you communicate and interact with others properly? You basically ask someone something simple. "What time is it?" or "What grade are you in?" or "What's your teacher's name?"

Asking that one simple question can be the beginning of a really beautiful friendship. If you're a fairly shy person, then you have to give this a try. A lot of your friends and schoolmates are waiting for you to step outside of your comfort zone and communicate with them. Also, try to be yourself; don't try to copy someone else. Being yourself allows you to show off what your heart and soul are truly made of. You should also learn to appreciate your abilities. Personally, I can play guitar, I can play chess fairly well, I love writing, and I'm really interested in business and politics.

I found one of my abilities when I first started writing, and it was amazing. I was able to share my thoughts and feelings with other people by writing them down on a piece of paper. So discover your own skills and really develop them, because if you don't, then they'll be gone. Don't lose confidence or hope, whatever you do. Just try to stay focused and trust yourself, and one day, you'll shine bright with your ability, like a star.

Accept who you are and believe that you are destined for great things. Let nobody crush your dreams—that's the biggest thing I've learned. Don't let anyone call you stupid, dumb, or weird for staying true to who you are. Just think about yourself and all your enjoyable abilities, and say to yourself, "I'm word proof. I'm word proof!" If you don't like who you are—well, that's too bad, because you're stuck with yourself for the rest of your life, and you have to learn to love *you*. I love myself so much that I could smooch myself, and I will not let anyone or anything change who I am. Others may have said that I'm weird or ugly, but that doesn't matter. Don't mind what other people say; only be concerned with what you think about yourself.

If your peers tell you that you're weird all the time, that's actually a good thing, because weird people are always the most creative ones. Your opinions might be different from many other opinions when it comes to the shows you watch, the clothes you wear, or the way you think. But having a different perspective is a gift that will bring you lots of success, so be glad to be yourself.

You can make friends in a variety of ways; try joining a sports team, participating in social activities, or using the magical power of your smile. As they say, "Easy peasy, lemon squeezy." Humans are the only species who smile and laugh in response to happiness. Scientists say that smiling is good for your physical health too. It also helps your social skills, because when you smile at someone, he or she will feel good about you and may even consider starting a conversation—and that could be the beginning of a new relationship. So whenever you're feeling unhappy, a little smile can go a

long way toward cheering you up.

Failure

Now, at the end of the book, I would like to discuss about the importance and necessity of failure. What can I say? Well, the way I see it is, *failure* is just another word for *success*. You might think that's crazy, but let me explain. Without our failures, we would never reach our goals. You don't learn anything when you're on a winning streak; you have to lose at some point and then challenge yourself to figure out what you did wrong.

> *I've failed over and over and over again in my life. And that is why I succeed.*
> —Michael Jordan

You have to fail in order to understand what's keeping you from succeeding. Do you know what causes us to fail? Our mistakes. It's OK if you make mistakes—everybody does—but you have to be careful. You only live once, so don't make too many mistakes. And try not to repeat the same mistakes; otherwise, your life will be miserable. Failure makes us stronger and gives us a greater ability to confront challenges. All human achievements throughout history were made possible through people learning from their failures and trying again. So don't be afraid of failure. And always remember: *what doesn't kill you makes you stronger*!

Key Points of the Book

✓ Nothing is impossible! You can achieve anything you want if you just take tiny steps toward your goals. In fact, impossible is possible!

✓ When you say something is impossible, your brain gets the message that anything you might try to do is equally impossible. After that, your brain locks into that way of thinking, and consequently, you will never be able to act against your mind-set.

✓ You have to pretend that there is no such word as *impossible* in the dictionary of success.

✓ Everything that happens to us is the result of the way we think. Our thinking causes our actions, and our actions shape our destiny.

✓ A negative attitude will bring lots of frustration and awfulness into your life, and it won't only influence your future success, but it will also affect your psychological and emotional well-being.

✓ According to the law of attraction, when you wish for something badly and are really positive about it, you're on the right track, and the universe will therefore attract whatever you need to fulfil your dream.

✓ Remember that the cure is in your mind. Diseases can't last in a body that is controlled by a positive outlook. Medicines are important to fighting illness, but what matters more is your brain's ability to keep your spirits up throughout the healing process.

✓ It's essential for you to know your talents by the time you're a tween, because that knowledge will ultimately lead you toward your goals and, finally, to success.

✓ Never try to be like the average person, because being average is boring and lame, and it won't get you any success.

✓ Never let excuses take control of your mind and discourage you from following your dreams. You can even use those excuses like a turbocharger to propel you toward your dreams.

✓ Your current situation is the basis for your future, and when you try to be thankful for your current situation, you will then be able to achieve what you envision for the future.

✓ I don't know whether you've realized this fact or not, but in life, the more you give, the more you get. And the more grateful you are, the more you achieve.

✓ The law of attraction attracts everything that you can possibly imagine in your brain. And by *everything*, I mean everything.

✓ When you're trying to attract something, you have to act like a winner—act like a winner.

✓ The most important factor in finding any kind of success is thinking big.

✓ Always remember that nothing is impossible—you just have to believe that you can do it, take action, and move forward. So don't worry about the possibility of not reaching your goal.

✓ If you don't have any dreams, then you don't have any goals for your life—and in today's world, if you are living without goals, then your life is all about survival.

✓ Remember, when we achieve our goals, our self-confidence gets a big boost, like from a rocket. We all have only one life, so make sure that you live yours amazingly well.

✓ When you believe in a dream and invest your time and dedication into meeting it, well, guess what: "Your wish is my command." The law of attraction will find the easiest and fastest way to get you to that dream.

✓ The human brain has the ability to make things seem either bigger or smaller in our minds. Everything depends on our ability to control our brain.

✓ If you want to achieve big, then act big.

✓ Accept who you are and believe that you are destined for great things. Let nobody crush your dreams.

✓ Failure is just another word for success. Failure makes us stronger and gives us a greater ability to confront challenges.